THE THAMES

Daniel Rogers

Photographed by Isabel Lilly

Wayland

THE WORLD'S RIVERS

The Amazon
The Danube
The Ganges
The Mississippi
The Nile
The Rhine
The Seine
The Thames
The Volga
The Yellow River

Cover *St Pauls Cathedral rises up beyond the Thames in London.*

Series and book editor Rosemary Ashley
Series and book designer Derek Lee

First published in 1993 by
Wayland (Publishers) Limited
61 Western Road, Hove
East Sussex, BN3 1JD, England

British Library Cataloguing in Publication Data
Rogers, Daniel
Thames.—(World's Rivers Series)
I. Title II. Series
914.22

ISBN 0-7502-0429-X

Typeset in the UK by
Dorchester Typesetting Group Ltd
Printed in Italy by G. Canale C.S.p.A.
Bound in France by AGM

CONTENTS

1. 'OLD FATHER THAMES'

The Thames is not one of the world's largest or longest rivers. It is not even the longest river in Britain – the Severn is longer. However, it is one of the most famous rivers in the world. It was named Tamesis by the Romans and has been celebrated by minstrels and poets throughout history. The reason for the river's fame is the fact that it has played a vitally important part in the history of Britain.

The river existed before the beginning of the Ice Age, more than two million years ago, although its course was then further to the north than it is today. At the end of the last Ice Age, about 10,000 years ago, the Thames settled into its present course. Its route to the sea begins in Gloucestershire, in the west of England. The river then passes through Oxfordshire, Berkshire, Surrey and Greater London. Finally, the Thames flows into the North Sea in a long, wide estuary between Essex and Kent, in south-east England.

The sun sets behind Tower Bridge, one of the most famous landmarks on the Thames.

LEICESTERSHIRE
Leicester
0 10 20 30 40 50 km
0 10 20 30 miles
Birmingham
Coventry
NORTHAMPTONSHIRE
N
Warwick
Northampton
Cambridge
SUFFOLK
WARWICKSHIRE
CAMBRIDGESHIRE
BEDFORDSHIRE
Grand Union Canal
GLOUCESTERSHIRE
Cheltenham
COTSWOLD HILLS
OXFORDSHIRE
Cherwell
BUCKINGHAMSHIRE
HERTFORDSHIRE
Evenlade
loucester
Colne
Churn
Oxford Canal
Lea
Roding
ESSEX
Thames
Oxford
Lechlade
Thameshead
Abingdon
CHILTERN HILLS
Dorchester
Cricklade
Wallingford
Marlow
LONDON
Southend
Westminster
Canvey Island
Shoeburyness
Henley
Eton
Thames
Goring Gap
Maidenhead
Thames Barrier
Tilbury
Avon
Pangbourne
Windsor
Staines
Greenwich
Sheerness
Reading
Dartford
Kennet
Teddington
BERKSHIRE
Chertsey
Rochester
Kennet and Avon Canal
Maidstone
Mole
Medway
WILTSHIRE
HAMPSHIRE
Wey
SURREY
KENT
Salisbury
Winchester
Southampton
WEST SUSSEX
EAST SUSSEX
Brighton
DORSET
Portsmouth
Isle of Wight
English Channel

2. PHYSICAL FEATURES

From source to sea

Over the years there have been many arguments about exactly where the Thames actually begins. Some people have claimed that the river's source is at Seven Springs, near Cheltenham, while others have said it begins at Thameshead, near Trewsbury Mead in Gloucestershire. Eventually, in 1937, following a debate in Parliament, it was decided that Thameshead is the true source, and that Seven Springs marks the start of the River Churn, a tributary of the Thames.

The length of the river, from its source to the point at which it flows into the North Sea, is 352 km. Compared to some of the other great rivers of the world, the Thames is just a small stream. The Nile, for example, which flows through Egypt into the Mediterranean Sea, is 6,695 km long; the Amazon in South America measures 6,570 km from the headwaters of one of its main tributaries to the sea; and the combined Mississippi and Missouri rivers in the USA have a length of 6,019 km.

This small spring near Trewsbury Mead in Gloucestershire, is the source of the Thames.

An aerial view of the river to the west of London.

We do not know for sure how long the Thames has been flowing but it is likely that the river was in existence more than thirty million years ago. About two million years ago, the period known as the Ice Age began. The temperature fell and a vast sheet of ice spread from the north to cover much of Britain and northern Europe. Britain was joined to the rest of Europe at that time, and the Thames was a tributary of the River Rhine. During the Ice Age the climate occasionally became warmer for a time, and in those periods, lasting several thousand years, the ice sheet retreated.

Some 10,000 years ago, the Ice Age came to an end. As the ice melted the level of the sea rose, separating Britain from the continent of Europe and enabling the Thames to flow directly into the North Sea.

Along its course the Thames is joined by a large number of tributaries, the best-known of which are the Cherwell, Thame, Lea, Colne, Roding, Kennet, Mole, Wey and Medway. Some other tributaries, that once ran into the river in London, can no longer be seen on the surface although they still flow underground.

The Thames Basin – the area from which the river collects its water – is divided into two parts by a ridge of chalk through which the Thames flows at Goring Gap, near Reading in Berkshire. The river basin above Goring Gap consists of a number of valleys formed from soft clays and ridges made of harder sandstone and limestone. Below Goring Gap the river enters its lower basin, often called the London Basin, where the rocks are a mixture of chalk, sands, gravels and clays.

After flowing through London, the Thames marks the boundary between the counties of Kent and Essex. A short way downstream from Gravesend in Kent, the river enters its estuary. The land on both sides becomes flat and marshy. In some places the marshes have been drained to provide firm ground for building on. The mouth of the estuary, where the Thames flows into the North Sea, is marked by an imaginary line between Shoeburyness in Essex and Sheerness in Kent.

The drainage basin of the Thames covers a large part of southern England.

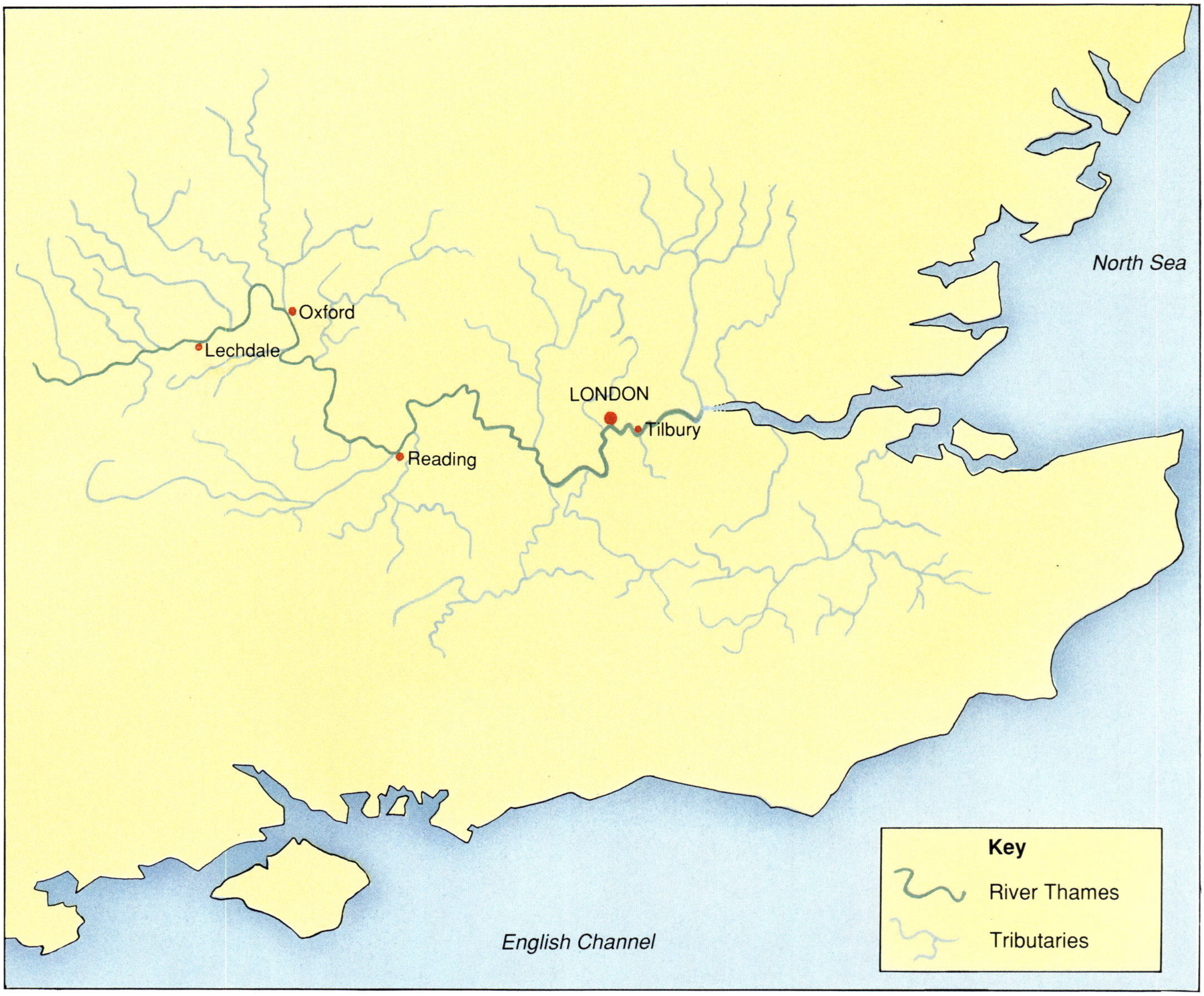

Above *On its journey through London, the Thames flows under more than two dozen bridges and passes through the commercial centre of the capital, the City of London.*

Left *Southend-on-Sea, in Essex, is a popular holiday resort on the north coast of the Thames estuary. The structure in the background is the pier, which is the longest in the world.*

Left *The weir at Marlow, Buckinghamshire. Weirs are designed to reduce the flow of water and make the river behind them deeper and more navigable.*

Right *The locks at Teddington, Surrey. Below this point, the Thames becomes a tidal river, and water from upstream mixes with that brought upriver by the tides of the North Sea.*

Controlling the river

Since Roman times, people have been building structures to alter the flow of the Thames. The first of these were low dams called weirs. The weirs were built downstream of shallow stretches and were designed to hold up the flow of the river to make the water behind them deeper. In this way, ships were able to sail through parts of the river that had previously been too shallow.

There are a number of weirs on the Thames, including King's Weir in Oxfordshire, Pangbourne Weir in Berkshire and, probably the best-known of all, the weir at Teddington, Surrey. More than 773,000 cubic metres of water flow over Teddington weir every day.

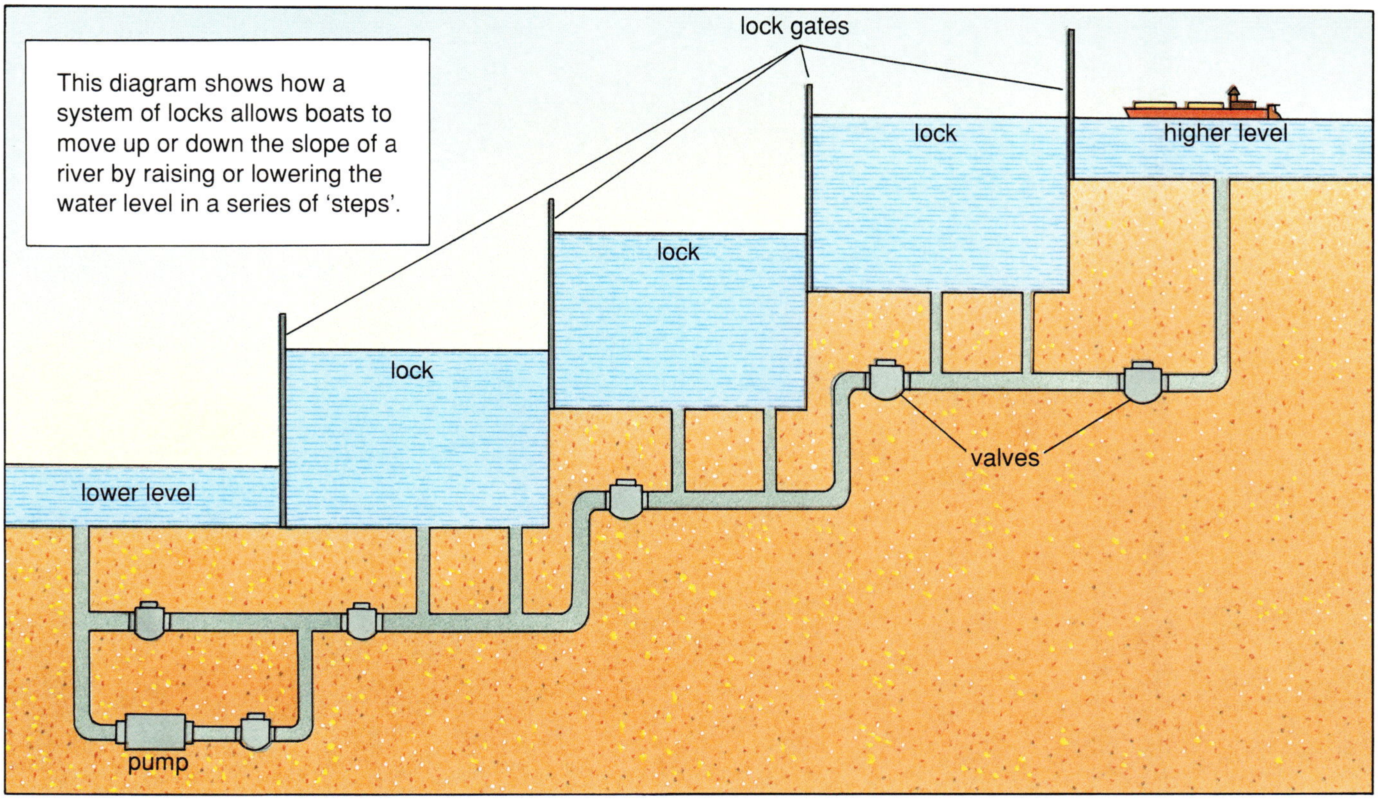

Above *A typical lock system.*

Below *Storms and high tides caused serious flooding in the Thames estuary in 1953.*

Another method of water control – locks – can also be seen at Teddington, just downstream of the weir. The locks at Teddington mark the point where the Thames becomes tidal. Locks are built to raise or lower the level of water in a river and enable barges and other boats to go up or down stream in a series of 'steps'.

Floods

From the very earliest times, the Thames has occasionally overflowed its banks, drowning people and livestock and damaging buildings. Such floods have occurred at points all the way along the valley, from the estuary to the highest reaches. Most of the time, however, the Thames is a gentle river, and this means that when floods do

Graham Hawes

'I am Operations Manager at the Thames Barrier. We have a workforce of eighty, and half of them are maintenance staff. I am responsible for overseeing the maintenance and testing of the barrier gates, and for supervising the river banks. The gates are closed once a week at low tide, for testing purposes. Once a year they are closed for a whole day for full tests. Checks are made for signs of wear and tear and to see how they stand up to the build-up of water. We usually do this around October, when we often have strong winds and high tides. In October 1991 we found that Gate C was slightly slow because of a build-up of silt.'

happen they always come as a surprise. One of the worst floods happened in 1894, after twenty-six days of heavy rain. A large area of the valley was submerged for many days. Floods caused by heavy rainfall are now much less common than they were, partly because better weirs have been built in recent years, and partly because the river bed is dredged more effectively.

In 1953, a fierce storm in the North Sea combined with an exceptionally high tide to cause a surge of water along the east coast of England and in the Thames estuary. In all, more than three hundred people were drowned.

The Thames Barrier

In order to prevent storm surges from flooding London, the Thames Barrier was built at Silvertown in 1982. When a surge threatens, ten huge steel gates can be raised from the river bed to hold back the water and prevent it from rushing upriver. However, the south-east of England has been tilting downwards very slowly, during the last 10,000 years, ever since the end of the Ice Age, and this means that the tides get slightly higher all the time. This, combined with the effects of global warming, means that by about the year 2030, the Thames Barrier may no longer be high enough to protect London.

3. THE THAMES IN HISTORY

Early settlers

Humans have lived in the Thames Valley for thousands of years. Archaeologists have found stone tools which suggest that the first settlers may have arrived as far back as 300,000 years ago. These tools include axes and sickles made from pieces of flint and polished stone.

When the last Ice Age ended, about 10,000 years ago, Mesolithic (or Middle Stone Age) people began to move into the valley. They were rather more advanced than the earlier settlers, and were able to make a wide range of tools and weapons. They lived in tribes of about eighty people, and survived by hunting, fishing and gathering wild plants and berries. The tools they made helped them to carry out these tasks and to cut and shape timber to build their wooden dwellings.

Around 2400 BC, came the start of the Bronze Age, named after the metal

An archaeological dig at Swanscombe in the Thames Valley and (inset) a Stone Age flint axe-head that was found at the site.

This late Stone Age pottery beaker was found in the Thames at Mortlake, Surrey.

which was first produced at that time. Bronze is a mixture of copper and tin, which were mined in the parts of Britain now known as Cornwall and North Wales. At first, bronze was expensive and was only used to make jewellery and weapons. Gradually, as it became more widely available, the metal was used for farming tools and many other everyday objects. The remains of Bronze Age settlements have been found at Bray, Egham and elsewhere in the Thames Valley, together with metalwork and pottery from the period.

During the Bronze Age, trade began between Britain and the continent of Europe and the Thames Valley became a leading trading area, with manufacturing centres being established along the river. New inventions and manufacturing methods from Europe appeared in the valley earlier than in other parts of the country.

From about 800 BC, iron began to replace bronze as the most important metal. Iron was in abundant supply in Britain and its use spread widely. Although bronze continued to be used for making jewellery and other costly items, iron is a stronger metal and it became widely used for tools and weapons. Sometime after 800 BC – no one is sure exactly when – Celtic people from Europe crossed the English Channel and invaded Britain.

It seems that the Iron Age was not a peaceful time. Many defensive hillforts were built, especially in southern England. They were intended to protect various Celtic tribes and settlements from attack by each other, and were strongly fortified with a series of circular earth banks, ditches and wooden palisades. Despite the warring among the Celts, long-distance trade continued to grow and the people living in the Thames Valley prospered.

Part of a Celtic shield found in the river.

Invaders

After about 250 BC, more and more of the imports to Britain came from a new source – Roman Italy. As the power of Rome grew, its armies spread outwards and eventually conquered an empire larger than any the world had seen before. Britain, and especially the rich area of the Thames Valley, attracted the Romans and, in 55 and 54 BC, their emperor, Julius Caesar, launched raids against the south-east of England.

In AD 43 the Romans began a full-scale invasion. After landing in Kent, their army reached the crossing point of the River Medway without much resistance, but at that point they were met by a large British force. The resulting battle, which lasted for two days, was won by the Romans who then advanced to the Thames and awaited the arrival of their emperor, Claudius. After his visit, the conquest was resumed and most of England and Wales came under Roman control.

The Romans are well-known for their skill in road-building, but they were also good at constructing river transport systems: they built wharves where goods could be loaded and unloaded, strong barges which could carry large cargoes, and bridges where rivers could be crossed. They were the first people to build a bridge across the river at

Above right *A bronze head of the Roman Emperor Hadrian, which was found in the Thames at London Bridge.*

Right *The Normans built a number of castles in the Thames Valley in order to strengthen their hold on the country. Rochester castle in Kent is one of the best remaining examples.*

Londinium – the Roman name for London – the town they established on the north bank of the Thames. Londinium became the capital city and major seaport of the new Roman province of Britain. Another important Thames bridge was built at Staines, known as Pontes in Roman times.

From about AD 370, the Romans' hold on Britain began to weaken, as peoples called Picts and Scots invaded from the north and Saxons from northern Europe attacked in the south. Around 410, the last Roman troops left Britain. The Saxons pushed into the Thames Valley and established hamlets along the river banks. Names of towns ending in 'ing', such as Reading, are reminders of the Saxon period.

The coming of Christianity

In 597 St Augustine landed in Britain, having been sent by Pope Gregory to convert the people to Christianity. Soon, great monasteries were built along the banks of the Thames at Westminster, Chertsey and Abingdon, and a cathedral was constructed at Dorchester, where the River Thame flows into the Thames.

The peace that Christianity had brought to the country was shattered by the raids of Viking peoples from Scandinavia. At first they came simply to steal as much gold and other valuables as they could carry away in their longships, but gradually they began to settle in Britain. By 870 they had sailed up the Thames as far as Reading, although the Saxon king, Alfred, later pushed them back. After Alfred's death, in 899, the Vikings, or Danes as they were known, stepped up their raids, and by 1016 Britain was ruled by a Danish king, Cnut.

The Norman Conquest

In 1066 yet another invading army attacked Britain. The Normans under William of Normandy sailed across the English Channel from northern France and landed at Pevensey on the south coast of England. After defeating the English at the Battle of Hastings, William took control of the Thames Valley and then the rest of England. In order to strengthen his rule and to subdue the revolts which broke out during his reign, William built many strong castles, including those by the Thames at Windsor and Wallingford, and at Rochester and the Tower of London.

The Norman Conquest was the last time that invaders set foot in the Thames Valley. However, the river continued to play a central role in the history of Britain. One of the most important events that took place along the banks of the Thames was the signing of the Magna Carta (or Great Charter) at Runnymede in Surrey, on 15 June 1215. King John was forced by his nobles to sign the Magna Carta, which was intended to ensure that the king treated his subjects fairly and justly; it marked the start of democracy in England. During the Middle Ages, between about AD 1000 and 1500, the Thames continued to be a vital route for the movement of goods and people, and a number of market towns, such as Henley and Lechlade, grew up beside the river.

Defending the river

Even though there were no further invasions, the Thames remained a target for would-be attackers, and so it was heavily defended. In 1539, during the

The Tower of London

This famous fortress was begun by William the Conqueror soon after his arrival in Britain, in 1066. He built the fortress to guard access to the Port of London and as a means of controlling rebellious citizens. The central keep, built of white limestone from Normandy and known as the White Tower, was begun in 1078. The fortress was later extended and surrounded by a moat which was fed by the Thames.

For centuries the Tower was used as a state prison. Prisoners entered through 'Traitors' Gate', the river entrance to the Tower. Many brought there were murdered, or were executed on Tower Green or in public on nearby Tower Hill. Two well-known victims were the boy-princes, King Edward V and his younger brother, who were mysteriously murdered in the Tower in 1483.

The Tower is still guarded by yeoman warders or 'beefeaters' and the crown jewels of Great Britain are kept there.

reign of Henry VIII, a fort was built at Tilbury, on the river's estuary, to repel invading ships. Elizabeth I strengthened the fort and it was there that she rallied her troops when they were faced with the threat of attack by the ships of the Spanish Armada in 1588. Early in the nineteenth century, England feared an invasion by Napoleon, who had gained control of France after the French Revolution of 1789-99. A network of forts was built to defend the Thames and many can still be seen today.

Until the mid-nineteenth century, the Thames in London was broad and fairly shallow. Because of this, the river often froze over in severe winter weather. From about the 1860s, the river was made narrower and deeper by dredging and the construction of stone embankments, so that large trading ships could sail into the heart of London.

Frost fairs

When the Thames froze over, in severe winters, frost fairs were held on the ice, with market stalls, fairground amusements and performing bears. People rode from one bank to the other in horse-drawn carriages. The last frost fair was held in 1814. Ice no longer forms on the river, mainly because the climate is warmer, and also the river is deeper because of dredging.

4. TRANSPORT

Early river craft

The first boats seen on the Thames, about 10,000 years ago, were probably rafts consisting of a number of logs tied together, and dug-out canoes. Rafts were probably used for carrying people and their possessions along the river, while canoes were more useful for fishing.

During the Neolithic (or late Stone Age) period, techniques for making flint tools improved greatly and the tools would doubtless have been used to cut and shape tree trunks for boat-building. River craft of that time were probably flat-bottomed punts, resembling rafts with raised sides and ends. The timbers of these boats would have been tied together with thongs (strips of animal hides). Later, during the Iron Age, longer-lasting iron fastenings were introduced.

When the Romans invaded Britain, they introduced more advanced boat-building techniques and constructed strong barges which were able to carry large loads to and from the farms, villages and potteries along the banks of the Thames. In the ninth century, the Vikings arrived with their long, narrow

River traffic on the Thames at Greenwich in the eighteenth century.

Thames sailing barges were once used to transport goods along the river.

ships made from overlapping wooden planks. The ships used for sailing upriver were about 12 m long, were driven by oars 3 m in length and steered by means of a rudder or 'steerboard' hung from one side.

The trading route

During the Middle Ages, England became very wealthy through the export of wool, which was among the best in Europe. As in many other parts of the country, farmers in the upper valley of the Thames kept large flocks of sheep and sent their wool to market by river. In fact, nearly all England's woollen cloth exports passed through London. Some towns in the valley became extremely wealthy thanks to the wool trade; Lechlade in Gloucestershire is one example, with its imposing church built with money from the sale of local wool.

London also benefited from the export of wool, as the city taxed all woollen cloth passing through. From about the fourteenth century, London profited from another trade – cargoes of coal. This fuel was brought from the north-east of England in ships called colliers, which sailed up the Thames to unload their cargoes in London. This coal was also taxed.

Canals, barges and tugs

Coal was brought to London by sea because, in the days before good roads and railways, that was the only way of transporting bulky cargoes. In the eighteenth and early nineteenth centuries, barges became increasingly important as a huge network of canals was constructed in Britain. The canals were built to link major towns, industrial areas and rivers, and enabled goods to be carried throughout the country by barge. By 1830, when the last canals were built, Britain had 6,500 km of navigable inland waters. Not surprisingly, some of these canals were linked into the Thames – most notably the Kennet and Avon Canal between Bath and Reading, the Oxford Canal linking the Midlands to Oxford, and the Grand Union Canal joining Brentford to Birmingham.

Thames barges carried bricks, cement, timber, malt, grain, flour and manufactured goods. Another important cargo was hay; in the days before motor vehicles were invented, horses were a vital form of transport and vast quantities of hay were needed to feed the nation's horses.

Some barges were driven by sails, while others were towed along rivers and canals either by horses or by teams of men. Sometimes as many as eighty men were needed to pull a 200-tonne barge. The horses or men walked along towpaths beside the water and pulled the barges along by means of ropes. Later,

These modern barges are carrying waste to be dumped in the North Sea.

Tilbury is now one of the most important docks on the Thames.

barges were towed by steam tugs and, most recently, by petrol- or diesel-powered tugs. The rapid development of the railways from the mid-nineteenth century onwards, together with improvements in the quality of roads, took most of the traffic away from Britain's inland waterways.

London's docks

Barges carrying goods for export, and trading ships sailing into and out of the capital, docked at what was called the Pool of London, just below the Tower of London. By the end of the eighteenth century, the Pool was far too small for all the ships that wanted to use it – in 1794 a total of 3,663 ships came into the port of London, more than three times the number that arrived at the beginning of the century. To cope with this increased traffic, and with the fact that ships were becoming larger and larger, a network of new docks was built. First, in 1802, came the West India Docks on the Isle of Dogs, and they were followed by the London Dock at Wapping – much closer to the city – and the East India Dock on the Isle of Dogs. St Katherine's Dock, opened in 1828, was the closest to the heart of London. It was carved out of a densely populated area near the Tower of London and 11,300 people were evicted from their homes to make way for its construction.

In 1866, a brand new dock was built on the Thames at Tilbury, on the marshes of Essex, more than 40 km from London. At first, very few ships would use the new dock because of its distance from the capital, but gradually it grew in importance. From the 1950s onwards, when more and more cargoes began to be shipped in sealed metal containers, Tilbury's role grew even more rapidly. Furthermore, ships continued to get bigger, and only Tilbury and other estuary ports had enough room to expand to accommodate the larger vessels. These big deep-water docks continue to thrive, as large ships are still the cheapest way of transporting bulky cargoes over long distances.

As the docks nearer to London lost trade to Tilbury and other container ports,they started to close down and by 1981 they were all shut. In the 1980s and early 1990s, these largely derelict docklands were developed for other uses. Giant office blocks were built to attract business from the overcrowded City of London and expensive blocks of flats and marinas for pleasure boats were constructed. As a result, London has ceased to be a port, and the Thames now carries very little commercial traffic.

Right *Thames barges in the Pool of London, 1962. Since this photograph was taken, the old London docks have all closed down and there is now very little commercial traffic on the river.*

Left *A pleasure cruiser carrying tourists on a sight-seeing trip. Much of the river traffic on the Thames today consists of pleasure boats and sailing dinghies.*

Paul Brookes

'I am the skipper of this cruise ship, the *Abercorn*, which is owned by Catamaran Cruisers in London. I have worked on boats up and down the river all my working life. My father was also a skipper and my brother works for the same company. I usually take the boat from Charing Cross to Tower Hill and down to Greenwich, but I prefer working upriver, around Hampton Court. The *Abercorn* can carry 276 passengers and I give them a running commentary about the Thames – I have taught myself a lot about the history of the river. The *Abercorn* was built in 1924 and has appeared in films and TV shows.'

There are still boats and ships on the river, although many of them are pleasure craft which carry people on sight-seeing cruises up and down the river. Each year many thousands of tourists visit London and the Thames Valley, and a large number of them go for a trip on the river. Some pleasure boats have restaurants and discos to entertain their customers, while others are simply water taxis. There are also more than 30,000 cabin cruisers, dinghies, canoes and flat-bottomed punts which are used purely for recreation.

Riverboat Disasters

From the early nineteenth century, when pleasure boats became popular on the Thames, there has been a conflict between people who want to enjoy themselves on the river and those who see it as a place of work. The most recent example happened in August 1989 when a large freighter, *Bowbelle*, collided with the pleasure boat *Marchioness*, which sank with the loss of more than fifty passengers who were attending a party on board.

An even greater disaster had occurred in September 1878 when a paddlesteamer, *Princess Alice*, was hit by the *Bywell Castle*, a collier ship. The *Princess Alice* was wrecked and 640 people were drowned; bodies were washed up by the tides for weeks afterwards.

5. CROSSING THE THAMES

Fords, bridges and ferries

For many centuries, the Thames was an important transport route. However, it has also acted as a barrier. Today there are many bridges spanning the river, but before they were built people had to find a fording point – a place where the river was shallow enough to wade across. Towns and villages grew up near these fording points, and they can still be identified by their names; Shifford, Duxford, Oxford and Wallingford, for example. Later, boats were used to carry people and goods, including livestock, across the river.

Newbridge, near Oxford, was built in 1250 and later rebuilt during the fifteenth century.

In time, people learnt how to construct bridges to enable them to cross the river. The first major bridge across the Thames was probably built by the Romans in London. It would have been constructed from timber, which has since rotted away over the centuries. However, archaeologists now believe they have found some evidence that such a bridge existed. After the Romans left Britain, in AD 410, their bridge almost certainly fell into disrepair; it was not replaced until 1209, when a stone bridge (known as Old London Bridge) was built. A number of other bridges were built across the Thames during the Middle Ages, including those at Wallingford in 1141, Windsor in 1268 and Abingdon in 1416.

The bridge at Wallingford, Oxfordshire. It was here that William the Conqueror and his army forded the Thames after invading Britain in 1066.

Old London Bridge

London's first stone bridge was begun in 1176 and took thirty-three years to build. It was a huge structure, with nineteen stone arches supported by massive wooden piers, or 'starlings'. Although the bridge was only 6 m wide, wooden shops and houses were perched on top of the arches. From 1305, the heads of executed criminals and rebels were displayed on poles set up on the bridge. Despite this gruesome custom, which lasted until 1678, the bridge was a very fashionable place on which to live.

Old London Bridge effectively stopped ships from sailing up the Thames because the arches were too small for most vessels to pass through. There was a small drawbridge in the middle which could be raised for larger ships, but the flow of water between the starlings was very fast, and 'shooting' the bridge (sailing through the arches) was dangerous for boats of all sizes.

Old London Bridge was not the only means of crossing the river in London. Some Londoners crossed by ferries, at Lambeth and Fulham. The wealthiest inhabitants could afford their own river barges, but most people travelled in small boats rowed by 'watermen', who gathered at the foot of the many flights of stone stairs which led down to the river.

Meanwhile, the streets of London were becoming crowded with horse-drawn carriages, which were first introduced in 1565 and threatened the watermen's trade.

The watermen tried to prevent the building of other bridges in London. However, in 1729, London's second bridge was completed at Fulham despite their objections. A number of other bridges followed, including Westminster Bridge in 1750, Hammersmith Bridge – London's first suspension bridge – which opened in 1827, London Bridge, which

Right *The two towers of Tower Bridge are over 60 m high and 60 m apart.*

Below *The Queen Elizabeth II Bridge at Dartford, which was opened in 1991.*

Above *This ferry carries people across the Thames between Windsor on the south bank and Eton on the north.*

replaced Old London Bridge (demolished in 1831), and Tower Bridge, one of London's most famous landmarks, which was opened with great ceremony in 1894. The most recent bridge to be built over the Thames is at Dartford, Kent, and was completed in 1991; it carries the M25 motorway that follows a circular route around London.

Tunnels

In addition to the bridges over the river, tunnels have been dug to carry traffic underneath it. The first Thames tunnel was built by the famous engineer Isambard Kingdom Brunel at Rotherhithe in 1842. At first it was more of a tourist attraction than a useful means of crossing the river, but in 1862 it was sold to a railway company and eight years later the first trains ran through it. Since then, many other tunnels have been built to carry road traffic, railways and underground trains beneath the Thames.

Below *Road bridges and tunnels that cross the Thames in London.*

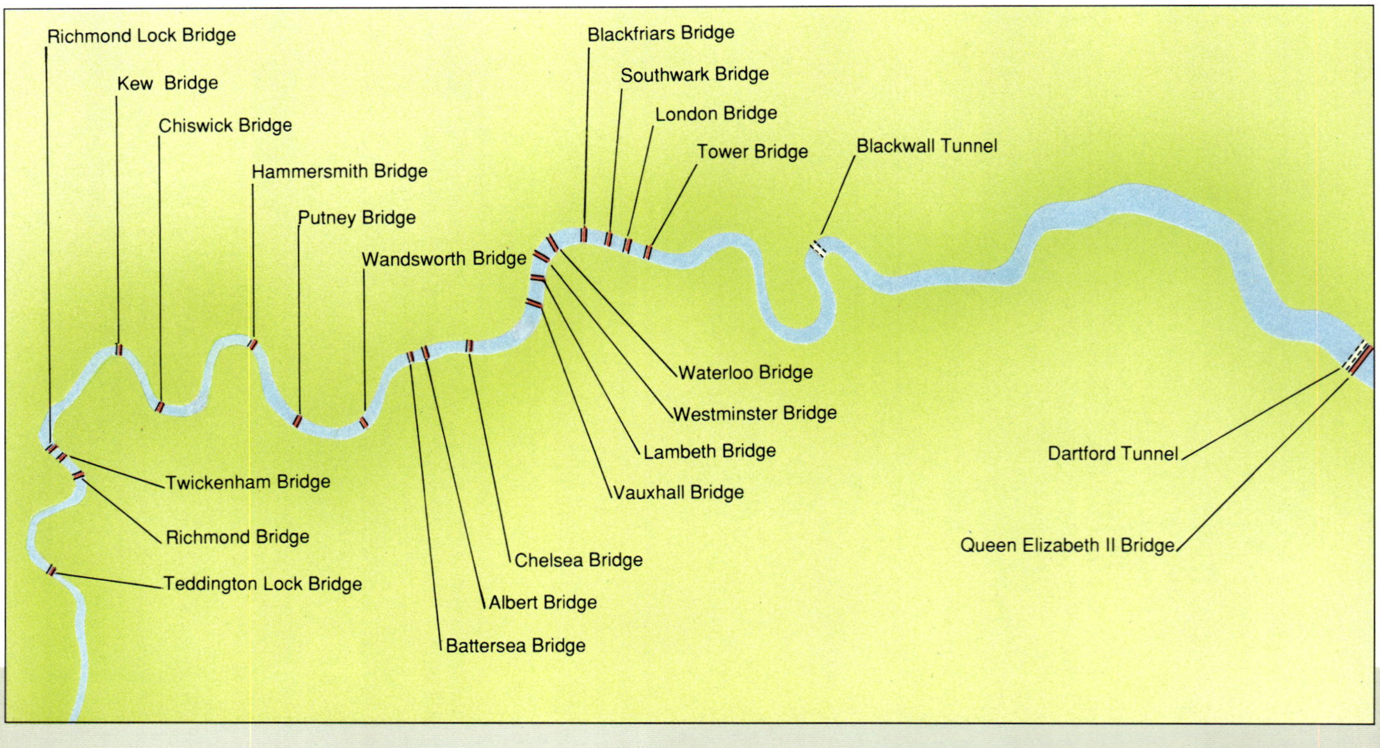

6. AGRICULTURE IN THE THAMES VALLEY

People have lived in the Thames Valley for about 300,000 years. The first inhabitants lived by hunting, fishing and gathering fruits and seeds from wild plants. The first farmers arrived around 6,500 years ago, during the Neolithic period. They made good flint tools that enabled them to cut down large areas of the natural forest, which then covered most of Britain. They cut down the forests to produce fields in which they grew wheat and raised livestock, especially cattle and sheep.

They usually cleared areas of forest close to the river, and some of these cleared areas were farmed continuously for several centuries. As farming techniques improved – especially with the introduction of the first simple plough – the land was able to provide food for more people and settlements became larger. Trading networks grew up between the settlements, and the Thames became an important waterway for transporting goods.

The coming of the Bronze and Iron Ages brought better tools, which enabled people to clear the forests more easily and create networks of small, straight-sided fields. The land was very fertile and allowed people to grow more food than they needed; the surplus was traded with other communities as far away as Spain and Scandinavia. When the Celts arrived in Britain, around 800 BC, they brought with them improved farming methods and soon put much of the best land – including that of the Thames Valley – under the plough.

Britain was a province of the Roman Empire from AD 43 to 410. During that time, its population was increased by the large number of soldiers in the occupying army and the people who ruled the province. A great deal of food had to be grown to support these people, and many

An Iron Age Farmstead

Although many large hillforts were built during the Iron Age, it is thought that they were used only in times of danger, when enemies threatened to attack. Most of the time, people lived in their own small farmsteads. Each farmstead consisted of a large circular hut inside a compound, surrounded by a wooden palisade. Around the compound were fields, some of which were fenced in to prevent cattle and sheep wandering off, and others in which cereals and other crops were grown.

The picture shows a reconstruction of an Iron Age hut.

farms grew up in the Thames Valley. Cereal crops such as wheat were very important, and some farms grew up to 200 hectares of the cereal.

In the fifth century, large numbers of Anglo-Saxon people came to Britain from Scandinavia and northern Germany. They built thousands of small villages throughout England. The villages usually had large open fields around them, cleared from the natural woodlands. These fields were divided into strips of land that were cultivated by the villagers.

Following the Norman Conquest of 1066, more of the natural woodlands of the Thames Valley were cleared so that the fertile land could be put to good use for agriculture. Some of the forests that lay beside the river were preserved for William the Conqueror's favourite pastime – hunting.

During the Middle Ages, some of the small plots of land that were typical of Saxon England were combined to make larger fields. Often these were turned over to livestock farming – especially sheep farming, which was very profitable

Cattle grazing on water meadows beside the river near Wallingford, Oxfordshire. The Thames Valley is a very fertile agricultural region.

Stephen Cook

'This farm has been in my family for over thirty years. The Thames runs through my fields and in the old days the valley was often flooded, so the soil is very fertile. I grow winter wheat, barley, oil-seed rape and hay in my fields. Although the land is fertile it tends to dry out easily if there is no rain. I don't plough the land up to the river banks, but I use these water meadows beside the river for grazing cattle.'

because English wool could fetch a high price abroad.

The process of making farms and fields larger and larger has continued up to the present day. In many places, the types of farming carried on have changed little over the centuries – sheep are still raised on pastures in the upper valley of the Thames, while further downstream much of the land is used for growing cereals, especially wheat and barley. An aerial view of the valley today shows a land that is rich in crops but, apart from the towns, almost empty of people.

Sheep have been raised in the Thames Valley for centuries. There are far fewer of them today than during the Middle Ages, when wool was a very important export.

7. TOWNS AND VILLAGES

Along most of its course, the Thames is lined with fields. At intervals, however, towns and villages have been built on the banks. Some of these settlements are very old indeed, and most owe their existence to the Thames.

Moving downstream from the river's source, the first town to be reached is Cricklade. This small town dates back at least to Roman times when it was known as Dobunni. It was important in Saxon times, when it had its own mint for

A view over the rooftops of some of the famous university colleges in Oxford. The first college was established here in the mid-thirteenth century. The city now attracts thousands of tourists every year.

Part of the historic town of Abingdon, once the site of an important abbey.

producing coins. Further downstream is Lechlade, which was a bustling market town in the Middle Ages. The skyline is still dominated by its church, built in 1470 from the profits of the wool trade.

The first major settlement along the river is the city of Oxford. The city dates back at least to the fifth century, when Saxons settled there, and its name comes from the fact that it was the first place at which the river could be forded by oxen. However, the area to the north of Oxford may well have been occupied since the Bronze Age or even earlier. Today, Oxford is most famous for its university – the oldest in England – but it was a flourishing market town long before the first college was built in 1249.

The town of Abingdon is located at what has been an important crossing point of the Thames since Stone Age times. The first bridge was built there in 1416, in order to lure away some of the trade that passed through Wallingford, which had its own bridge. Abingdon once had an important abbey – one of the richest in England – but it fell into ruins after King Henry VIII closed down many of England's monasteries in the 1530s.

The small town of Dorchester was built at the point where the Thames is joined by one of its tributaries, the Thame. In Roman times it was an important settlement. It was here that a Christian missionary called Birinus converted the Saxon King Cynegils and baptized him into the Church, an event which helped to spread Christianity through England. Dorchester became an important religious centre, but it lost its prominence in the eleventh century when its bishop moved to Lincoln.

Left *Rowers practising on the river at Henley. Each July, Henley hosts a world-famous rowing regatta.*

Right *Windsor Castle dates from 1070. It was largely rebuilt during the reign of Henry II (who died in 1189), and has been altered several times since then. It is now one of the most popular tourist attractions along the Thames.*

Wallingford, downriver from Dorchester, is now a small market town. But long ago it was one of the most important towns in England. It was originally a fording point, and the Saxons later built a bridge there; after the Roman bridges at London and Staines had decayed, this was the only one across the Thames. Wallingford was a military stronghold in the early Middle Ages, but was then overshadowed by Abingdon and Oxford.

Reading is another town that dates back to Saxon times. Nowadays it is an important business centre and a major centre of communications, with roads, railways and the river all meeting there. Further on is Henley, which was a medieval market town but is now best-known for its annual rowing regatta held every July. Maidenhead was a crossing point in the Stone Age, and it now has two bridges spanning the Thames. The road bridge, completed in 1777, carries traffic on the route from London to Bath; people using it were forced to pay a toll (fee) until 1903, when the toll-gates were torn down and thrown into the river by angry local residents. The other bridge was built in 1838 by Isambard Kingdom Brunel, to carry the Great Western Railway.

The Tate Gallery – one of the most famous of London's many art galleries.

Downriver is Windsor, which has the largest castle in the world. The first structure on the site was a Norman fort, built in about 1070. There was major rebuilding in the twelfth century and in the 1820s and '30s. The town of Windsor grew up at the foot of the castle. Just across the Thames is Eton, home of the famous public school, and a short distance downriver is Runnymede, where the Magna Carta was signed in 1215.

The largest town along the Thames is, of course, London. The first settlement on the site was the Roman city of Londinium, on the north bank of the river. At that time the city was very small, even though it was the capital of the Roman province of Britain. London grew rapidly during the Middle Ages and became the country's most important trade and administrative centre.

Today, the area known as Greater London covers 1,580 sq km and has a population of more than 6,700,000. The so-called City of London, which is on the site of the old medieval city, is one of the world's major financial centres. During the day it is full of people working in offices and banks, but at the end of the working day it becomes almost deserted, as fewer than 5,000 people live there. London is England's main cultural and entertainment centre, with countless theatres, cinemas, art galleries and restaurants. It is also the seat of government; the Houses of Parliament – especially the clock tower of Big Ben – are world-famous landmarks on the Thames.

The Houses of Parliament and the clock tower of Big Ben. The name Big Ben actually refers to the large bell which sounds on the hour. Although the Houses of Parliament look very old, they were constructed between 1840 and 1860.

8. INDUSTRY

Fishing

Ever since the first human settlers arrived in the Thames Valley, the river has been fished to provide a source of food. By the Middle Ages, a sizeable fishing industry had developed, and some people were worried that so many fish were being caught that the supply might run out. This did not happen, however, and fishing was still an important industry on the Thames in the early nineteenth century. In those days, there was a wide variety of fish to be caught, including sole, cod, herring, sprats, flounder, eels and even salmon. Salmon was much sought after because it fetched a high price at market.

Although fishing is no longer an industry on the Thames, people still fish for pleasure.

The Kennet and Avon Canal, which links the towns of Bath and Reading.

Fish catches – especially of salmon – started to fall in the early nineteenth century. This was partly because of the building of new locks and weirs, which prevented fish from making their way upstream. A more important reason was the increasingly widespread use of the flush toilet. This device enabled huge quantities of sewage to be poured into the sewers of London, from which it eventually found its way, untreated, into the Thames. This caused a massive increase in pollution and killed many of the fish in the river.

Until quite recently, it was thought that the Thames was too dirty and polluted for any fish to live in, at least in London. A great effort has been made to clean up the river and some fish have now returned.

Other industries and tourism

Many of the industries that now flourish along the banks of the Thames do not owe their existence directly to the river. During the last fifteen years, part of the Thames Valley has became an important centre for the manufacture of high-technology electronic equipment – especially parts for computers. These industries were established in the valley because of the vital communications network that has developed there. Motorways, other major roads and railways all radiate outwards from London to other parts of Britain, and some of them follow the Thames Valley for at least part of their route. Furthermore, London's major airport, Heathrow, lies to the west of London

within easy reach of firms based in the valley.

Along most of the Thames, the factories that have been built in riverside towns tend to be engaged in light industry. In Reading, for example, brewing and biscuit-making industries are important, as well as light engineering, including electronics and service industries, such as banking and insurance, tourism, hotels and catering. Other towns in the valley also concentrate on light industry and services.

Most of the heavy industries in the area are to be found between London and the sea. In the Thames estuary, for example, there are large docks, oil refineries, power-stations, cement factories and heavy engineering works. London itself has a huge range of industries, although there is now little heavy engineering. It is perhaps most famous as one of the world's major financial centres, with interests in banking, insurance, foreign currency exchange and dealing in company stocks and shares.

Throughout the Thames Valley, one of the major industries is now tourism. Each year, millions of visitors travel to Oxford, with its beautiful and historic university colleges, to Windsor Castle and, especially, to London, with its endless list of attractions. All these tourists need hotels and other places in which to stay, food to eat, petrol for their cars and much more, and the money they pay for all these provides a living for thousands of people living around the Thames.

Above *Most heavy industries, such as this oil refinery on Canvey Island, Essex, are located in the estuary between London and the sea.*

Above right *Lloyds Building, in the City, houses London's international insurance business.*

Right *Hampton Court Palace was built in 1551 by Cardinal Thomas Wolsey and later became a royal palace. Today it is a popular tourist attraction.*

9. ENVIRONMENTAL PROBLEMS

Pollution

During the last two hundred years, one of the most important problems facing the Thames has been pollution. Yet, even in the early 1800s, the problem was not a new one: in 1297 the Earl of Lincoln complained that water from the Thames in London was undrinkable because of the filth poured into it from tanneries.

Pollution again became a serious cause for concern in the first half of the nineteenth century, with the rapid increase in the use of flush toilets. Although they were first invented in the sixteenth century, they did not come into widespread use until the 1800s. Previously, people had used chamber-pots which they emptied into cesspits. The cesspits were then emptied by

This engraving from 1844, shows the River Fleet. The Fleet once flowed through London and joined the Thames; it now runs underground. The pipes coming from the houses and factories on either side discharged untreated sewage and other waste directly into the Fleet. The waste was then carried into the Thames, from where some of London's drinking water was taken.

A water pumping station in Surrey. Water is pumped from the Thames and passed through filter-beds (which look like ponds) to remove some of the impurities. It is then purified further before being piped to homes, offices, schools and factories.

'night-soil men', who took the contents away to use as manure for the market gardens which supplied London with fresh vegetables.

Cesspits could not cope with the large quantities of water and waste produced by the introduction of flush toilets; sewers were needed. However, there were no proper sewers and so raw sewage was simply passed, untreated, into the drains designed to carry away rainwater from the streets. These drains led directly into the Thames – often within a few metres of the pipes through which drinking water was taken out of the river.

Later in the nineteenth century, many other sources of pollution were added, most notably the filthy waste poured into the Thames by the gasworks which produced fuel for London's gas lighting. Other factories added their own poisonous substances to the already foul mixture.

Drinking water

In the previous chapter we saw how pollution affected the fish in the Thames; its effects on public health were equally disastrous. At the beginning of the nineteenth century, London's population was almost one million, and more than half the drinking water for the capital was taken directly from the Thames. This water was not given any treatment to make it clean. Instead, it was stored in tanks, first by the water companies that pumped it from the river, and then by people in their homes. By the time it was eventually used it was in a worse state than when it had been taken from the Thames.

In 1832 there was an outbreak of cholera in London which is thought to have killed 5,300 people. Although no one knew it at the time, cholera is caused by drinking polluted water. Further cholera epidemics broke out in 1848-49,

1853-54 and 1866. Eventually, towards the end of the century, scientists discovered the link between the disease and the quality of drinking water. Around the same time, a more modern system of water supply was established with efficient water treatment plants, and taps, baths and wash-basins in people's homes. Even so, sufficient water was not always available and it was not until 1899 that most Londoners had constant running water in their houses.

The quality of the water improved slightly up until the 1920s. But between then and the late 1930s, the population of London almost doubled in size with the building of new suburban areas surrounding the capital. The sewage treatment works intended to cope with the waste from these areas were not very effective, and so river pollution increased again. To make matters worse, during the Second World War (1939-45), German bombs destroyed many sewage pipes and by the 1950s the Thames was more polluted than ever before, with sewage and with industrial waste.

A survey at the time found that there were no living fish in the 77 km stretch of river between Kew and Gravesend.

Water on tap

Today, the majority of people living in the Thames Valley still get their water from the river. Thames Water, the company that supplies it, is the largest water authority in the world. It is responsible for an area of 13,000 sq km, with more than 2,500 km of rivers and water courses and over 90 water treatment works. Each day, it pumps over 4,500 million litres of water to the homes, offices, schools and factories in its area through a network of 42,000 km of water mains.

Cleaning the river

Attempts to clean up the Thames began in the mid-1960s, when sewage works were improved and efforts were made to reduce pollution flowing into the river from factories. As a result, fish have now returned to the river – so far, 109 different species have been found.

Many kinds of wildlife have returned to the Thames since the clean-up began in the 1960s.

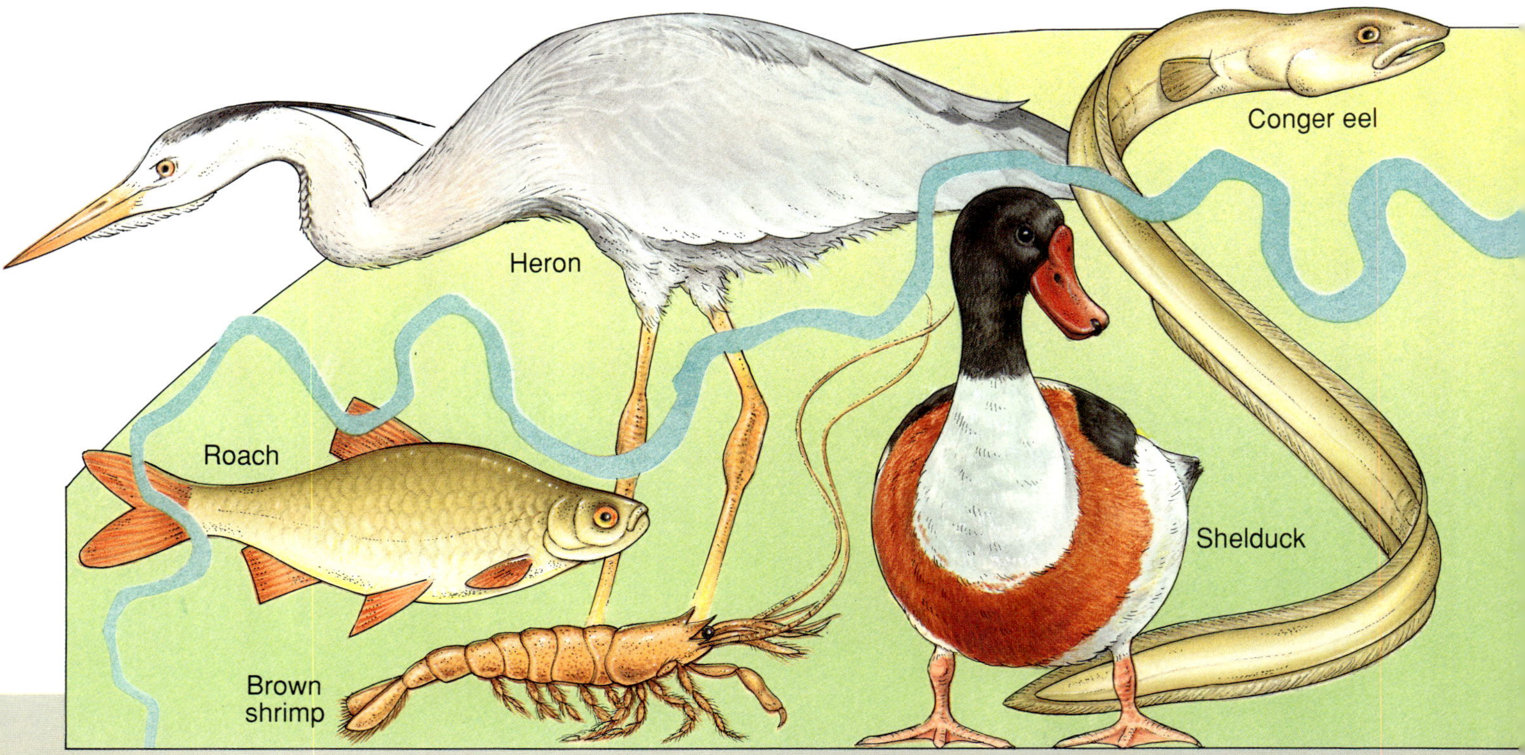

Above *Construction work is underway to develop the old docklands into a business and residential area.*

There are still pollution problems facing the Thames. Vast quantities of fertilizers and pesticides are used by farmers on their fields in the Thames Valley to improve their crop yield. When these chemicals wash through the soil and into the river they can poison fish and other wildlife. Nevertheless, the Thames is cleaner now than it has been for centuries.

Alan Cooper

'I am a Pollution Officer for the National Rivers Authority. I spend most of my time checking water quality, either by land or by water. I do a weekly boat trip to check the river between Richmond and Southend and test the water around sewage works and major industrial sites that are discharging into the Thames. I take samples of the water and test them in the floating laboratory for 'suspended solids' (sewage) and harmful chemicals. We also have special surveys to test for heavy metals such as copper, zinc, lead, nickel, cadmium and mercury. Four times a year we do an 'estuary run', from Richmond to the estuary; generally the lower and upper reaches of the river are the cleanest.'

Demolition and redevelopment

Another important issue emerged during the 1980s. It concerned the docks rather than the river itself. When the old docks of London began closing down in 1967, at first they were left to become largely derelict. Then, in 1981, they were handed over to the newly formed London Docklands Development Corporation. Since then, the old wharves and warehouses have been demolished to be replaced by new office blocks and expensive, fashionable houses and flats to accommodate wealthy people from the City of London. The remaining inhabitants of the old dockland communities were outraged; graffiti appeared reading 'Hands off our Waterfront' as well as other, more aggressive slogans.

The development went ahead despite these protests, and without many of the planning and building restrictions that affect other projects. Docklands is now a maze of buildings in a mish-mash of different styles. It has far more office space than is needed and some office blocks are less than half-full. The future of the development became uncertain in 1992, when the property company responsible for a large part of the project appeared to be in danger of going bankrupt with debts of almost £7 billion.

10. THE FUTURE

We have seen, in previous chapters, the changes that have taken place along the Thames from the earliest times to the present day. But what is likely to happen in the future?

The changes that occur will probably be small and gradual. For example, there is little doubt that the Thames Valley will continue to be an important farming area, even though some land will be taken out of agricultural use to cut down on the surpluses of certain foods that are at present being grown. A small amount of farming land may even be used for building new towns.

Many of the existing towns along the valley will continue to grow. London will remain the cultural, business and administrative capital of England and the popularity of the Thames for tourists should increase. This will help to provide work for more and more people.

Hopefully, the river will continue to become cleaner as greater efforts are made to prevent pollution. However, there is a threat from the large quantities of artificial fertilizers and pesticides which have been spread on the farmland in the valley over recent years. These chemicals sink through the soil into the groundwater below the surface and eventually find their way into rivers, killing fish and other water creatures.

The days when the Thames was a busy commercial river are now gone. Cargo ships load and unload at Tilbury and other docks near the estuary, and most goods travel up and down the Thames Valley by road and rail rather than by river. Between its source and London, the many beautiful reaches of the Thames will remain a playground for people in small boats and a source of pleasure for walkers, anglers, artists and many others.

Swans and ducks on a tranquil reach of the Thames.

GLOSSARY

Archaeologists People who study ancient buildings and objects.
Barges Flat-bottomed boats used for transporting cargoes on rivers and canals.
Canal An artificial waterway.
Celtic people (Celts) People from central and southern Europe who settled in Britain more than two thousand years ago, before the days of the Roman Empire.
Cereals The general name for grain crops, such as wheat, rye, barley and oats.
Cesspit A covered tank for collecting and storing sewage and waste water.
Cholera A severe stomach illness caused by drinking water infected with a certain type of bacteria.
Containers Large metal boxes, made in a number of standard sizes, for carrying cargoes. Containers can be easily transferred between lorries, docks and ships.
Democracy A government that is run by the people of a country or by their newly elected representatives.
Derelict Falling into ruins.
Dredge To remove mud and silt from a river bed.
Embankment An artificial bank of earth or stone designed to prevent a river from flooding.
Estuary The area in which a river widens as it approaches the sea.
Fertile Able to produce good crops.
Global warming The increase in the average temperature of the earth caused by the build-up of gases in the atmosphere which slow down the escape of the sun's heat from the earth.
Graffiti Drawings and messages scribbled on walls of public places.
Hamlets Small villages.
Headwaters The streams flowing into a river near its source.
Ice Age A period in which the climate is much colder than normal and the polar ice caps extend over a far greater area. The last ice age ended about 10,000 years ago.
Locks Sections of a canal or river that may be closed off to control the water level and the raising and lowering of boats that pass through.
Navigable A waterway that is wide enough or deep enough for boats to sail through.
Neolithic The period known as the late Stone Age, from about 4000 to 2500 BC.
Palisades Strong defensive fences made of stakes driven into the ground.
Sewers Underground drains or pipes, used to carry away surface water and waste matter (sewage).
Starlings The piers built up from a river bed to support the arches of a bridge.
Surplus An amount left over after using what is needed.
Suspension bridge A bridge that hangs from rods attached to cables which are supported by towers on either side.
Tanneries Places where animal hides and skins are made into leather.
Tidal Relating to the flowing in and out of the tide.
Tributary A river or stream that flows into a larger river.
Tugs Boats with powerful engines for pulling barges and other ships.
Weirs Artificial barriers built across a river to reduce the flow.
Wharves Platforms of wood, stone or concrete built at a harbour or on a river bank to enable ships to dock or load and unload cargo.

BOOKS TO READ AND ADDRESSES TO CONTACT

Books

Great Britain by Andrew Langley (Franklin Watts, 1990)
Past into Present AD 43-1400 by Christopher Culpen and David Linsell (Collins, 1992)
Rivers by Terry Jannings (Oxford University Press, 1990)
The Thames by Charles Lyte (Wayland, 1980)
The Thames Barrier (National Rivers Authority, 1992)
Water for Life by Philip Parker (Simon and Schuster, 1991)

For older readers

London by Barnaby Lenan (Collins, 1992)
London River by Gavin Weightman (Collins and Brown, 1990)

Addresses

The Museum of London
London Wall
London EC2Y 5HN

The National Maritime Museum
Park Row
Greenwich
London SE10 9NF

The Thames Barrier Visitors' Centre
1 Unity Way
Woolwich
London SE18 5NJ

Picture acknowledgements
All photographs are by Isabel Lilly except the following: Cephas/Nigel Blythe 4, 27 (top); C. M. Dixon 13 (both), 14 (both), 15 (top), 23 (top), 29; © Michael Holford 25; Hulton Picture Co. 11; Tony Stone Worldwide/Ian Murphy cover; Topham 20, 21, 24 (lower); Wayland Picture Library 18, 19, 26 (lower), 40. The map on page 5 is by Peter Bull Design. Artwork on pages 8, 11, 28 and 42-3 is by John Yates.

INDEX

Numbers in **bold** refer to illustrations